LOOK AHEAD

a guide to
working in...

Healthcare

Jeremy Wallis

www.heinemann.co.uk
Visit our website to find out more information about **Heinemann Library** books.

To order:
- ☎ Phone 44 (0) 1865 888066
- 🖹 Send a fax to 44 (0) 1865 314091
- 💻 Visit the Heinemann Bookshop at www.heinemann.co.uk to browse our catalogue and order online.

First published in Great Britain by Heinemann Library,
Halley Court, Jordan Hill, Oxford OX2 8EJ,
a division of Reed Educational and Professional Publishing Ltd.
Heinemann is a registered trademark of Reed Educational & Professional Publishing Ltd.

OXFORD MELBOURNE AUCKLAND
JOHANNESBURG BLANTYRE GABORONE
IBADAN PORTSMOUTH NH (USA) CHICAGO

Designed by Ambassador Design Ltd, Bristol.
Originated by Ambassador Litho, Bristol.
Printed in Hong Kong/China

ISBN 0 431 09480 2
04 03 02 01 00
10 9 8 7 6 5 4 3 2 1

British Library Cataloguing in Publication Data
Wallis, Jeremy
   A guide to working in health care - (Look ahead)
   1.Medical care - vocational guidance - Great Britain
   I. Title II.Health care
   362.1'02341

Acknowledgements
The Publishers would like to thank the following for permission to reproduce photographs:
Allsport, pp. 24/Paul Severn, 39/Mark Dadswell; John Birdsall Photography, pp. 30, 40, 45; John Walmsley, p. 21; Network, pp. 14, 17/John Cole; PA Photos/Rebecca Naden, p. 8; Rex Features/Adrian Dennis, p. 26; Robert Harding Picture Library, pp. 15, 10/R. Grey/Shout; Science Photo Library, pp. 18 Stevie Grand, 22, 37/Hattie Young, 28/Juergen Berger/Max-Planck Institute, 33/Hank Morgan, 35/Geoff Tompkinson, 43/Deep Light Productions, 47/Matt Meadows/Peter Arnold Inc; Wellcome Trust Medical Photographic Library, p. 12.

Cover photograph reproduced with permission of Robert Harding.

Our thanks to Joanna Dring, careers co-ordinator, Banbury School, Oxon for her help in the preparation of this book.

Every effort has been made to contact copyright holders of any material reproduced in this book. Any omissions will be rectified in subsequent printings if notice is given to the Publisher.

Contents

Technical words, jargon and specialist terms are explained in the glossary.

Working in healthcare

Want to work in healthcare? This book examines careers in hospitals, the community, public health, research, mental health and complementary medicine. It looks at the work of physiotherapists, dentists and dieticians. It also describes the qualifications and qualities needed by a healthcare professional.

The National Health Service

The National Health Service (NHS) was established in 1948 to provide free healthcare for all. It employs 1 million people, and spent over £42 billion in 1997/98 – the equivalent of more than £1700 a year for every household in the country! There is also a thriving private healthcare sector. The NHS is funded mainly by the taxpayer. Private healthcare is usually paid for through private medical insurance (PMI). More than 7 million people now have PMI cover.

What is the healthcare sector?

When an emergency is reported – a fire, train crash, natural disaster – we are familiar with dramatic images of health workers going about their duties. Working in healthcare can be exciting, but it's not always as TV dramas and newscasts show. We get a better impression from documentaries: on children's hospitals, the work of health centres, on innovative surgery and cutting-edge therapies. Many of us visit hospital or attend as patients, and the doctor's surgery is as familiar as the library or school.

However, our impressions are only snapshots of the healthcare system. Medically trained personnel are found everywhere – from hospitals to the work-place, health centres to health education campaigns, the armed forces to the merchant navy, research laboratories to sports injury clinics.

There are professionals who ensure our teeth, eyes, muscles and minds are healthy; experts in antenatal and post-natal care; in heart, lung, brain and intestinal medicine; in cancer and infectious diseases. Nurses tend the young, the old, people who are mentally ill and patients in intensive care. Plastic surgeons rebuild the features of people after surgical procedures and dermatologists help patients recover from skin damage. Physiotherapists work with injured athletes or accident victims. Psychiatrists and psychologists help people cope at home, work or school. Therapists use drama and art as remedies for depression and anxiety and language therapists work to restore the power of speech. There are also complementary practitioners – osteopaths, homoeopaths, acupuncturists. Supporting all these are: scientists and statisticians investigating the causes of disease, research organizations unravelling the enigma of our genes, doctors developing new treatments for victims of strokes, Alzheimer's disease or spinal injury.

In hospital trusts, health authorities and health centres, managers administer an army of staff – from porters, lab technicians, hospital DJs and chaplains to caterers, accountants, cleaners and personnel officers – ensuring everything runs smoothly.

On a typical day in UK healthcare ...

... 700,000 people visit their family doctor, 130,000 visit the dentist, more than 130,000 are treated in hospital outpatient clinics, pharmacists provide 1.5 million items on prescription, 2000 babies are delivered.

... 540,000 people receive NHS help in their homes, district nurses make 100,000 visits, chiropodists provide 6000 sessions in patients' homes.

... surgeons perform around 220 hip operations and 750 heart operations, ambulances make 8000 emergency journeys, around 10,000 people donate blood.

Types of contract

Hospitals and health centres need to have trained staff ready for every eventuality, and most are employed on permanent contracts. However, even after recent government attempts to raise wages, pay often compares badly with other sectors and there are staff shortages. In nursing, the deficit is eased by hiring nursing agency staff on short-term contracts. These might last from one shift to several weeks. An advantage of agency work is that a nurse can tailor work to fit other commitments to their family and so on.

Research is supported by both public and private organizations. Research scientists are often given a contract and a grant for a project which might run for several years. Hospital doctors are employed directly by the NHS while most general practitioners (GPs) are self-employed partners in a practice. (Many specialists treat private as well as NHS patients.) There are also locum doctors who provide cover for doctors who are on leave, undertaking training or sick. (Yes, doctors do get ill sometimes, too!)

Opportunities to work abroad

The skills of British doctors, scientists, nurses and other professionals are respected all over the world. Some countries, like the United States, offer generous salaries to overcome their own skill shortages. Many medical personnel work in developing countries, often for organizations such as Voluntary Service Overseas (VSO) and Médecins sans Frontières.

Getting the best from this book

This book is a beginning. It might trigger ideas or inspire you to follow a particular direction. But be warned: a career in any field of healthcare is hard! Furthermore, for aspiring doctors, entry to medical school is incredibly difficult and you must be sure of your commitment and be realistic about your abilities.

- Training is intensive. Qualification takes years and medical staff need to follow continuing medical education throughout their working lives.
- Hours can be long and unsocial. Enormous discipline, energy and mental toughness are required.
- While financial rewards for a GP or specialist are good, for many others they are poor. Few people work in medicine because of the salaries.
- The NHS employs many women. They form 78 percent of non-medical staff and 45 percent of general managers, but currently there are few women in senior management positions.
- Ethnic minorities are not yet well represented at senior medical and consultant levels. This is gradually changing as a broader social mix is being recruited into medicine and healthcare.

Working in hospitals

Things have changed a lot since people went to their barber for surgery, fortunately for us! Today, nothing symbolizes healthcare more than a modern hospital.

The Hippocratic Oath

The core of modern medicine – observation and the interpretation of physical evidence – was devised by Hippocrates, a Greek doctor, in the fourth century BC. He also wrote a code of medical ethics, the Hippocratic Oath, parts of which are still used today.

Hospitals concentrate resources and expertise, and train health professionals. Many pioneer unique care: Papworth Hospital in Cambridgeshire is famous for heart surgery, Great Ormond Street Hospital in London for treating sick children.

⭐ *Great Ormond Street Hospital in London specializes in treating children.*

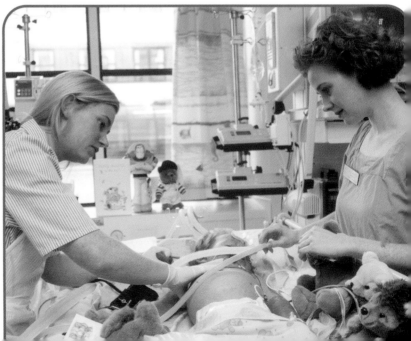

Becoming a **doctor** involves years of study. Medicine is so complex it needs more than physicians with a general medical knowledge. The focus is on specialization. Doctors who want to concentrate on psychiatric medicine, first qualify as medical doctors, then work for two years in other areas of medicine. Qualification as a **psychiatrist** requires three more years of study, followed by further training.

Many other professionals work alongside doctors. Best known are **nurses**. Grades range from **care assistants**, **staff nurses** to **nurse specialists** and **senior managers** with clinical responsibilities. Nurses initially train for 18 months in a common foundation programme, followed by an 18-month branch programme in adult, mental health, learning disability or children's medicine. After state registration, many specialize. An **ophthalmic nurse**, for example, provides support for eye clinics, wards and operating theatres.

While nurses in the community keep more conventional hours, nurses in hospitals must be ready to work shifts, often through the night, at weekends and during public holidays.

With sirens wailing and lights flashing, ambulances are a familiar sight on our streets. More recent developments include the motorcycle-mounted **paramedic** and the helicopter ambulance. Not so long ago, the job of an **ambulance crew** was to 'swoop and scoop' – get a casualty to hospital as quickly as possible. However, the condition of patients often worsened and many died. Doctors realized survival chances were massively improved if patients were treated soon after falling ill or being injured – in the 'Golden Hour'. Today's emergency crews will stabilize a casualty at the roadside or at home before taking them to hospital for further care.

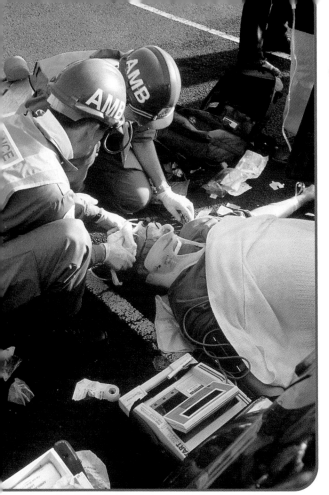

⭐ *Paramedics stabilize a patient at the roadside before taking him to hospital.*

In a major emergency, services are organized through an on-site **accident and emergency coordinator,** according to preparations based on regular 'major incident' rehearsals. The first task is to treat the injured. Accident and emergency (A & E) consultants and doctors may be flown in to work alongside paramedics.

Because illness often has long-term effects, many people are employed in professions allied to medicine (PAMs) to help patients (and families) cope. **Physiotherapists**, **speech** and **language therapists**, **psychologists** and **psychotherapists**, **occupational therapists**, **dieticians** and **nutritionists** assist in treatment, and enable patients to regain mobility or manage the new circumstances of their lives. We look at many of these careers in more detail.

Social workers are also employed to help people deal with the practical problems of hospitalization, for example by supporting families when a parent is ill.

CONSIDER THIS...
Interested in the emergency services? How about a career in the fire brigade or the police?

Because many modern procedures are technical, hospitals employ **biomedical scientists**, **medical physicists**, **medical laboratory assistants (MLAs)** and large numbers of specialist technicians. **Medical photographers** often record surgical operations; while they must understand the equipment, they must also be able to watch: no surgeon wants a photographer fainting onto the patient! Plastic surgery departments also employ photographers; some procedures require many operations over several years, and a photographic record is vital.

Almost all hospitals have a medical imaging department. **Diagnostic radiographers** use X-ray machines or scanners to examine the skeleton, muscles and organs of the body. **Therapeutic radiographers** treat diseases – principally cancers – by using focused radiation to destroy malignant (cancerous) tissue or cells.

As well as medical staff and technicians, few hospitals could operate without armies of **catering staff**, **cooks** and **canteen managers** and **porters**. Overseeing the whole institution is a **management team**, dealing with budgets, staffing issues, IT, payroll, external and internal communications and the organization of care within the hospital.

The NHS operates a training scheme to recruit and prepare graduates for management posts throughout the health service. The first part of the course involves a tour of the NHS, doing anything from shadowing an ambulance team to observing in an operating theatre. There are placements in other organizations, and trainees spend time running departments and units such as Outpatient or Mental Healthcare Centres.

Basic training and specialization

Training to be a doctor

Because commitment starts before medical school, it is important to study sciences like Chemistry, Physics and Biology that are the basis of the medical school curriculum.

Most colleges offer integrated courses. Students study anatomy, physiology, biochemistry, psychology, medical sociology and basics of pathology and pharmacology. In hospitals they are attached to a 'clinical firm' – usually two **consultants**, two **specialist registrars**, a **senior house officer** and a newly qualified **house officer.** This is the student's first introduction to patients.

After medical school, graduates work for a year in a General Hospital as house officers then register with the General Medical Council (GMC). They are now eligible to practise as doctors. But ... just when you thought that was it, there are thousands of specialist career paths that can be followed. Doctors must opt for one within two years of graduation.

⭐ *These medical students are attending a Biology class.*

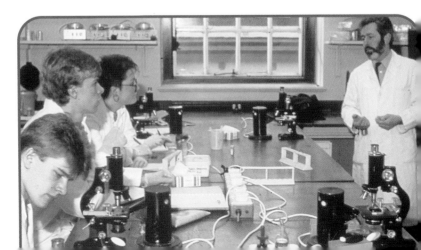

Nursing and midwifery training

There are two routes to obtaining a nursing or a midwifery qualification: a diploma or a degree programme. Both routes include supervised nursing practice in hospital and in the community as 50 percent of the training. Each course begins with an 18-month Common Foundation Programme (CFP) followed by 18 months in adult, mental health, learning disability or children's nursing. After qualification and state registration, nurses can follow a number of specialist courses.

Because of the shortage of nurses, hospitals realize they must support new and existing personnel. Some rotate staff between nursing areas to allow them to develop experience. Nurses are also being given more responsibility.

Midwives support women giving birth; they check a baby's development in the womb, monitor the mother and offer antenatal counselling. They train to diploma or degree level, with the emphasis on practical experience of care for women and families. There are specialist courses after qualification including family planning and research. Because hospital and community midwifery services are integrated, midwives rotate between them. Community midwives are attached to GP practices and Health Centres.

Specialization

There are many specialist careers a doctor can follow: accident and emergency, cardiology, geriatric medicine, neurology, occupational medicine, obstetrics and gynaecology, dermatology, paediatrics, radiotherapy and oncology or medical research.

Philip – Student Nurse

It can be strange caring for a six-month old baby one day, and dealing with a strapping six-footer the next!

Philip Green recently completed his 18-month branch programme in children's health. Nurses' wages are rising and Philip might earn over £18,000 in the near future.

Kids are funny. They're so optimistic and so desperate to be well, just so they can get on with the rest of their lives. Sometimes, it makes me feel really humble.

Very young patients bring their own problems. We've got to communicate at a whole other level, and it's a skill in itself to accurately assess pain or discomfort. Children's nursing is also about dealing with parents, brothers and sisters as well as patients. It's a test of my communication skills to be sensitive to their needs and fears as much as my patients'.

With cases ranging from babies to adolescents, there's a wide range of drug dosage levels and also a lot to learn about the effects of drugs on children of different ages. Specializing in a branch like oncology (cancer care) also demands a high level of scientific understanding.

Children's health can be a heart-rending area to work in; I don't think there's anything more distressing than the idea of a life cut short when it's barely begun. At times like that, the support of colleagues is important. It's equally important to realize we're trained to deal with it, and I'd be no good to anyone, especially my other patients, if it stopped me doing my very best for them.

⭐ Nursing children requires special skills.

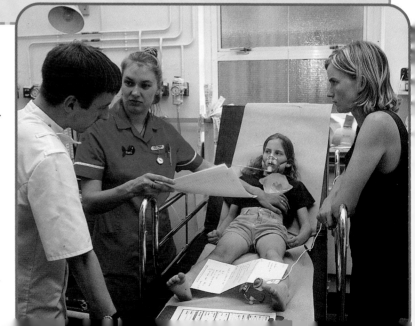

CONSIDER THIS...

INTERESTED IN A CARING PROFESSION BUT DON'T FEEL CUT OUT FOR NURSING OR MIDWIFERY? HOW ABOUT WORKING AS A:

- CARE ASSISTANT
- HOME HELP
- DENTAL NURSE
- HEALTH VISITOR
- VETERINARY NURSE
- NURSERY NURSE.

Surgery

As trainees, **surgeons** follow a Surgeons in Training Education Programme during their senior house officer rotations. They deal with open surgery and minimal access (keyhole) surgery, and learn the management of multiple injuries during the 'Golden Hour' (see page 9). Surgeons specialize according to their aptitude and interests. There are many specialities including vascular – dealing with arteries and blood supply – and neurosurgery – the brain and nervous system.

Peter – Anaesthetist

No one's woken up before time yet, so I'm doing something right.

As an anaesthetist, Peter Bostock uses drugs and machines to keep patients asleep during surgery. Peter currently earns around £32,000 per year. His salary will rise considerably with further experience.

Seriously though, most people know my job is to keep a patient unconscious or free from pain, and monitor breathing and vital signs. What many people don't realize is that we train as doctors before becoming anaesthetists.

In most cases the anaesthetist, having prepared the patient, decides when surgery can begin. I'm also responsible for blood transfusions, estimating blood loss and how much to replace. New anaesthetics have reduced the danger of reaction and many patients now leave hospital much sooner.

*Training is intense. We study the problems of different patients – children, elderly people, pregnant women – and anaesthetics related complications. As a **specialist registrar** I'm also trained to deal with new-born babies, cardiac surgery, and neurosurgery.*

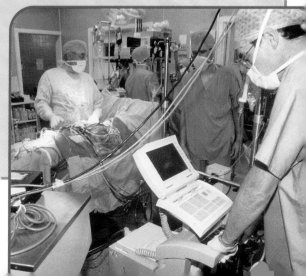

⭐ *This surgical team is performing a heart operation.*

Pathology

In the public mind, a pathologist is a nonchalant, scalpel wielding detective doctor up to his armpits in the chest cavity of a corpse. Reality is less dramatic, and such forensic pathology is actually the smallest branch. Pathologists study how diseases work, and are employed in every area of medicine. Pathology accounts for over four percent of health spending every year.

Most pathologists treat living patients. While some do post-mortems, most examine bone and tissue samples to help hospital clinicians and GPs diagnose and treat disease. Technological developments have also given pathologists knowledge of genetics and inherited disorders. The identification of genes which may predispose people to diseases like breast cancer and diabetes, means people at risk can avert illness by modifying lifestyle or diet.

A word of thanks ...

What have **pathologists** done for us? How about discovering penicillin, eradicating smallpox, diphtheria and polio in Britain, and developing vaccines for global killers like tuberculosis and malaria? Thanks to pathologists specializing in haematology (blood disorders), haematological cancers, such as childhood acute lymphoblastic leukaemia, are now curable in most cases.

Specializing as a nurse

Nurses also focus on particular areas and professional development is encouraged throughout their careers. At the University Hospital, Lewisham, in London, for example, the Dermatology Department has nurse-led clinics where nurse specialists take referrals from GPs, advise on treatment and provide care plans.

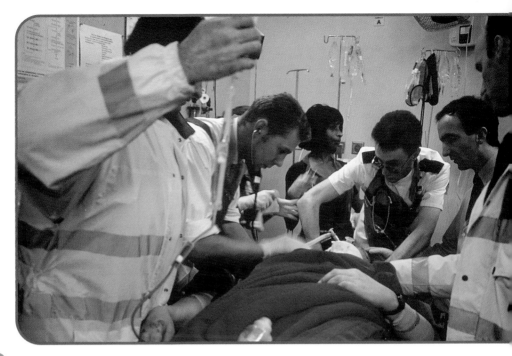

Accident and Emergency Departments are open 24 hours a day, all year round. **A & E nurses** are skilled, adaptable and dynamic, and work well in a team. A & E departments also have **psychiatric nurses** to deal with mentally ill patients.

In Surgical Services, nurses are involved at every stage, including pre- and post-operative, emergency treatment and rehabilitation. Critically ill patients spend time in Intensive Care, reliant on the attentiveness of trained nursing staff.

Based in wards, nurses in Medicine deal with a range of conditions. Specialists include **Macmillan nurses**, who support people with cancer and their families.

Nurses in an Elderly Care Team understand illnesses that affect old people and rehabilitation programmes such as physiotherapy and occupational therapy.

Theatre, **anaesthetics** and **pain relief** nurses are involved in surgical operations. Pain Team nurses make ward rounds to review cases and provide pain relief. Theatre nurses work as anaesthetics nurses, runners, circulating nurses, and scrub nurses.

17

Technicians and laboratory staff

Hospitals and laboratories employ many technicians and scientists. These include radiographers, audiological and clinical scientists, biochemists, cytologists and molecular geneticists, clinical engineers, microbiologists, physicists, medical technologists, operating department technicians, pathology technicians, medical laboratory scientific officers, clinical laboratory support staff, orthotists and prosthetists. As research in electronics, nuclear physics, genetics and molecular biology brings new procedures and drugs, technical and scientific skills are becoming more important.

Being able to see inside the human body is a vitally important diagnostic tool. **Diagnostic radiographers** in an imaging department take X-ray photographs. Radiographers also use advanced scanning technology such as magnetic resonance imaging (MRI), computer tomography (CT) and positron emission tomography (PET) to examine the skeleton and muscles, heart and blood vessels and most other organs.

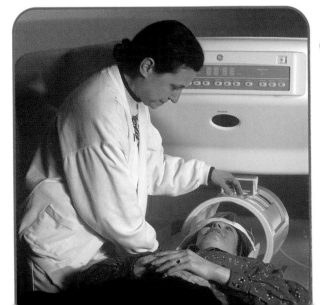

★ *The radiologist prepares a patient for scanning by an MRI scanner.*

Therapeutic radiographers use radiation to treat cancers. Tumours are subjected to precisely aimed and measured bursts of radiation, designed to destroy malignant cells without damaging surrounding tissue.

The development of new surgical techniques has increased demand for **technicians** to make sure they work. Keyhole and minimal-access surgery, for example, relies on endoscopic and microsurgical technology coupled to video screens and microscopes. Such small instruments and cameras require precise calibration.

I was working in the lab, late one night ...

Medical Laboratory Scientific Officers (MLSOs), often called biomedical scientists, diagnose disease, assess treatment and research causes and cures. Most specialize after basic training. Medical microbiologists isolate micro-organisms and examine antibiotics. Scientists in haematology study blood and haemoglobin, and those in transfusion science work in blood banks and the Blood Transfusion Service. Immunologists examine the immune system to identify conditions such as leukaemia, and test vaccines. Virologists detect viruses from HIV to influenza and screen for the strength of vaccines. In histopathology, biomedical scientists process tissue samples. Cytologists examine cellular material; best known for cervical smear tests, they actually examine a range of cells.

MLSOs work for hospitals, the Public Health Laboratory Service, the Medical Research Council, forensic laboratories, the Health and Safety Executive and the armed forces.

Many people who lose limbs because of accident or disease, wear false limbs or **prosthetics**. A new generation of artificial limbs in light, strong high-tech materials such as titanium and carbon fibre are being developed by prosthetists. They can be electronically triggered by nerve impulses and react to body movement. Joint surgery, such as hip replacement, is being improved by the use of new materials that allow the bone to form a strong bond with the artificial joint.

Working in
primary healthcare

The main focus of the NHS is now on primary healthcare teams based in medical practices or health centres. Members include general practitioners, nurses, health visitors, health professionals such as physiotherapists and speech therapists, and administrative staff.

General practitioners (family doctors) diagnose everything from anxiety to asthma and play an important role in preventative medicine. Almost half of qualified doctors become GPs. After registration, candidates follow two years of vocational training in hospital posts. Each of these posts lasts six months and they are usually specialities: paediatrics, obstetrics, psychiatry, geriatric medicine, accident and emergency. A year is then spent in general practice supervised by a GP trainer, seeing patients in the surgery and in their homes.

A **treatment room nurse** syringes ears, takes blood and dresses wounds. **Nurse practitioners** are trained to make basic diagnoses and can prescribe medication.

Health visitors are mainly concerned with preventing illness. They advise on child nutrition and check on infant development – measuring and weighing. If a child might be at risk of abuse or maltreatment, the health visitor liaises with child protection team members. Health visitors must first qualify as nurses before undertaking an additional course of study to become health visitors.

Martha – General practitioner

Describe an average day? I don't think I've ever had one.

Martha Mackenzie works in a busy inner-city practice in Birmingham. Martha earns around £45,000 per year. The salary structure is complicated and depends on the number of patients registered as well as procedures such as childhood immunization programmes, night visits, running clinics and so on.

We operate a walk-in surgery each morning. The first five patients yesterday were a case of high blood pressure, a woman with bronchitis, a widower with depression, a child with flu and a smoker with a persistent cough. I caught up with correspondence and made some home visits before lunch. I saw an elderly couple whose son has Down's Syndrome; they worry so much about what will happen to him they've made themselves ill. I also called on a patient with cancer.

During lunch we had an administration meeting and then I worked with a trainee GP in our 'lumps and bumps' clinic. We freeze off warts and other minor skin problems with liquid nitrogen, and refer more serious complaints to hospital.

My afternoon appointments were another mix of cases. Then I called in at our Carers' Group. People caring for sick or elderly relatives often feel very isolated. The Carers' Group is their opportunity to discuss problems with health professionals and meet others in a similar position.

⭐ General practitioners are usually our first contact with the NHS.

Julie – practice Nurse

I love the job. There's enormous variety, and I have lots of responsibility and independence.

Julie O'Connor works in a health centre in the south of England. As a nurse with several years experience, Julie earns £18,000 per year. Her wages are paid by the medical practice.

I used to work in a hospital but I have a family now, so working as a practice nurse suits me much better.

Every day is different. On a normal day I might change dressings, do smear tests, take blood samples and administer injections. The practice is also paid to assess new patients – looking at health, diet and so on.

Many women, and occasionally men, come for advice on contraception and family planning. With younger women, I also discuss issues around sexual health and lifestyle. It's made me very aware of the pressure on young women from TV, magazines, adverts and so on to conform to patterns of sexual behaviour from a very young age – and how important advice about contraception is.

I also help people control chronic conditions like diabetes or asthma. We review with each patient every six months. I take blood and weight, assess diet and recommend changes they might make. I occasionally do home visits to elderly patients.

I have a lot of responsibility and the doctors encourage that. It's a good working environment, and I'm part of a really supportive team.

⭐ *The nurse is administering a peak flow test to an asthmatic patient.*

District nurses visit people at home to administer medication, change dressings and ensure they are responding to treatment.

Clinical psychologists and **counsellors** are often employed to help patients with emotional problems, ranging from bereavement or relationship difficulties to depression.

Speech therapists and **physiotherapists** also operate as part of the primary healthcare team.

Chiropodists and **podiatrists** specialize in the care of feet. Many work in private practice, and many more are employed in health centres by the NHS. State registered chiropodists are trained to diagnose and treat a range of foot complaints and to correct or prevent foot disorders.

As well as medical staff, health centres employ administrative and practice development managers, receptionists and medical secretaries.

Support at the end

While our healthcare system is dedicated to keeping us well, death is an inescapable part of our experience. When an illness is too advanced to be treated, palliative care is given to alleviate symptoms and prevent unnecessary suffering. Many professionals work in hospitals, at home and in hospices to make terminally ill patients as comfortable as possible. Many conditions can be managed with medication, allowing patients to live their remaining days alert and pain free. Counsellors and therapists also help patients and their families cope with terminal illness.

Working in public health

Prevention is better than cure!

Amazing cures and surgical magic grab headlines, but more lives are saved through public health measures. These range from inoculation programmes to the reduction of disease by promoting healthy living.

The Health Development Agency maintains an up-to-date map of public health and health improvement. They commission research and advise on standards and health promotion practice. They also identify target groups for health promotion, distribute advice on good practice and carry out national health promotion campaigns.

⭐ *The serious and the fun runners must be very fit to take part in the London Marathon.*

Within health authorities, responsibility for public health rests with the Director of Public Health. **Public health doctors** are involved in the management of public health, communicable disease control and a range of public health and preventative health measures. They do not have a caseload of patients like a GP but they are, in effect, caring for everyone. For example, in the event of an outbreak of meningitis, they would be involved in containing it and establishing its origin.

A lot of public health work is epidemiological research where **statisticians**, **biomedical scientists**, **nurse researchers** and public health doctors chart how illness affects the population. **IT specialists** develop and maintain databases to map particular illnesses or the effectiveness of eradication programmes. Institutes of Public Health and the new Public Health Observatories in each NHS region monitor health and disease trends and highlight areas for action. The government now recognize that people without medical backgrounds also have an important role to play in public health. A broad range of skills allows for the development of partnerships with agencies and individuals.

Environmental health officers are employed by local authorities to protect public health. They ensure services such as sewers and drains are safe, and try to guarantee shops, restaurants and fast-food outlets maintain adequate levels of hygiene.

Because primary healthcare teams are an important part of any community, they also have public health functions. New responsibilities for **health visitors** include child health programmes, building support networks for example, to overcome social isolation for older people, advising breastfeeding mothers and women at risk of post-natal depression. Health visitors also identify the needs of homeless people and promote accident prevention.

Fashion victims

No one knew how extensive body piercing complications were, but GPs believed a problem existed and concerns were put to public health and environmental health officers.

A health authority in Lancashire carried out a study. It showed that 95 percent of GPs had dealt with piercing complications, including infections, blood poisoning, uncontrolled bleeding, disfigurement and even frostbite caused by using ethyl chloride to numb the area!

Four out of ten GPs had treated patients with pierced navels that went wrong. Other common problems included badly pierced tongues and nipples; one man had a stud put through the main vein of his tongue. Unable to stop the bleeding or remove the stud which was caught on a flap of skin under his tongue, he was rushed to hospital.

Those calling for regulation of body piercing were epidemiologists, who study diseases in the population at the Public Health Laboratories' Communicable Diseases Surveillance Centre, and environmental health officers.

⭐ *There are health risks associated with facial and body piercing.*

School nurses are ideally placed to help children, young people and parents. They provide advice on relationships and stress and can identify children who have missed the health service before starting school. School nurses can advise teachers, promote mental health in young people and provide advice on sex education.

Midwives target vulnerable groups such as young single mothers. They give advice for prospective parents on smoking, alcohol intake and diet and how these affect the health of the baby, and work with health visitors on post-natal depression, breastfeeding and how to best avoid cot death.

New technology also plays a part. NHS Direct, a 24-hour advice line staffed by nurses provides information on a range of illnesses. Internet help and advice sites are also being developed: NHS Direct On-line gives access to interactive self-care guides. NHSnet will link every GP surgery and hospital in the NHS.

CONSIDER THIS...

THERE ARE MANY WAYS TO MAKE A DIFFERENCE TO PUBLIC HEALTH WITHOUT WORKING DIRECTLY IN THE HEALTH FIELD.
- HOUSING OFFICER WITH A LOCAL AUTHORITY OR HOUSING ASSOCIATION
- TEACHER
- WELFARE RIGHTS ADVOCATE
- CITIZENS' ADVICE BUREAUX STAFF
- CONSUMER RIGHTS CAMPAIGNER
- TRADE UNION OFFICIAL

The Health and Safety Executive investigate work-place safety and prosecute negligent employers. They examine hazards, from the condition of a company's motor vehicles to the release of dangerous chemicals, and investigate accidents at work.

Occupational health deals with the health of people at work. Work-related injuries and diseases are a major cause of ill-health. Doctors or therapists examine illnesses such as repetitive strain injury or recommend action to ease stress at work. **Occupational psychologists** look at how people perform and behave in work and how organizations function. They also examine the effects of unemployment and the use of leisure time and retirement.

Working in research

Medical research is a rewarding, challenging and sometimes controversial area. Pharmaceutical companies use research to develop new treatments. There are privately funded research companies investigating human and animal genetics. Some health charities also fund research.

A lot of research in the UK is funded by the Medical Research Council (MRC). The MRC promotes research in all areas of medicine. Mainly funded by government, it is independent in its choice of research. The MRC has a world-wide reputation and is responsible for many medical discoveries.

A worm's eye view ...

In 1998, scientific history was made when British and American scientists announced the first complete genetic blueprint of an animal. The nematode worm, 1 millimetre long and containing fewer than 1000 cells, nevertheless has over 19,000 genes. The project to sequence its DNA took 15 years. 'So what?' you might ask. Well, the nematode worm is remarkably similar to us humans – 40 percent of its genes are related to ours! Researchers hope it will help identify genetic causes of human diseases.

⭐ *The nematode worm, shown here greatly magnified, is really only 1 mm long. It was the first animal to have its genetic blueprint completed by scientists.*

Clinical or biomedical science qualifications are not always essential for medical research. Many **social scientists** work on research projects. Epidemiology – the study of diseases in the population – is an area where social sciences, medical disciplines, statistics and mathematics meet.

Simon – Researcher

It's surprising how many social scientists build careers in health research.

Based in Edinburgh, Simon Burns is currently researching the public understanding of science. A researcher like Simon can earn over £20,000 per year.

There's a simple reason: a lot of healthcare provision is based on accurate analysis of delivery and costs. Because it's also about 'value for money', health economics is another huge growth area.

I intended to do Technology at university, but in my foundation year I did Social Sciences and really enjoyed it. I studied Sociology and then did a PhD in Science Studies and Science policy.

I often deal with questions natural scientists aren't equipped to ask. I recently looked at 'risk' – examining why people do things they know are dangerous. For example, you have to search to find someone who doesn't know smoking is dangerous, but people still smoke. Unprotected sex is dangerous, especially in high-risk groups, but people still take part in it.

Education in Britain is divided between natural sciences and social sciences. Recently, courses combining Natural Science and Sociology have started; they are good because they break down suspicions between natural scientists and the rest of us.

Caring for the mentally ill

Right now, one in six people are suffering some form of mental illness, from depression to schizophrenia. Contrary to the view sometimes given in the media, mentally ill people are more likely to harm themselves than anyone else. People with mental illness were once locked away in dreadful conditions. Today, we've moved to community based care. Health and social service staff work together in **community mental health teams** to provide a more co-ordinated approach. Most people with mental health problems are cared for by their GP, supported by community psychiatric nurses and other members of the primary health care team.

For every hundred individuals who consult their GP with a mental health problem, nine are referred for assessment by a **psychiatrist**. Most psychiatrists specialize in general adult psychiatry. They work in hospitals, people's homes and GP surgeries, alongside other professionals including nurses, social workers and psychologists. Some psychiatrists specialize in the mental health problems of children and young people, including those of depression, drug abuse and eating disorders.

⭐ With an ageing population, care of the elderly is becoming a more important field of mental healthcare.

In therapy

Some psychiatrists train as **psychotherapists.** Psychotherapists establish a relationship with the patient to help the patient deal with anxieties and change behaviour themselves.

Forensic psychiatrists deal with mentally ill people who break the law, in a variety of settings including hospitals and prisons.

People with learning difficulties can sometimes become depressed. Psychiatrists in **learning disability teams** work in special schools, hospitals, hostels and sheltered workshops.

Psychiatrists working with old people treat problems such as Alzheimer's or dementia. With 45 percent of the people in psychiatric units, and 25 percent of hospital admissions over 65 years of age, this is a growing speciality.

Psychologists also specialize in the mind, but are not medically qualified. **Clinical psychologists** teach stress management and social skills and detect anxiety, depression and behavioural problems. A **counselling psychologist** helps people to improve their sense of well-being, alleviate distress and resolve crises.

Educational psychologists examine learning and development and work with children, teachers and parents.

In addition to NHS Direct, there are help-lines offering advice on everything from alcoholism to bereavement. They include the National Schizophrenia Fellowship, the Samaritans and SANE. Many rely on non-professional staff, often volunteers, but a national organization like the Samaritans has a large training department.

Occupational therapy

The emphasis on care in the community has made occupational therapy one of the fastest growing areas of healthcare in Britain. It helps people live productive and independent lives. 'Occupation' isn't just work; it is any activity, from personal care to paid labour and leisure.

Occupational therapists work with people of all ages to overcome the effects of disability caused by psychological or physical illness, accident or ageing. Clients include people with Parkinson's disease, head injuries, motor neurone disease, strokes or learning disabilities. Elderly people often need help to live independently. Children are supported if they suffer from illnesses which affect mobility or fine motor skills. Occupational therapists also help people free themselves of the depression that can follow illness.

Occupational therapy (OT) focuses on everyday tasks we take for granted: washing, dressing, cooking and shopping. It helps people regain social skills and feel at ease with others. OT assists people return to work by building their confidence and advising on adaptations to the work environment.

Therapists also recommend practical adjustments to living environments; for example, suggesting equipment that enables an elderly person to live at home – walking frames, raised stools and bath seats, even long-handled weeders for garden lovers! OT might aid a child's co-ordination with special pencils and pens, and work with the teacher on the layout of the classroom.

Occupational therapists work in hospitals, research centres, disabled living centres, social services departments, mental health centres, the prison service, residential homes, hospices, charities and in an individual's own home.

Lynn – Occupational Therapist

Someone once said that every journey of a thousand miles starts with the first step.

Lynn Morgan works in a hospital in South Wales. Lynn is recently qualified and earns around £14,000 per year.

I work in a specialist therapy unit within the hospital. The team includes occupational therapists, physios, consultants and social workers.

There are lots of reasons a client might be admitted. Many elderly people come in after a fall, others with infections, or suffering from heart disease, arthritis or amputations. Everything is aimed at helping the patient lead as independent a life as possible. It might involve teaching self-care skills, providing wheelchairs and special equipment, giving advice on accident prevention. Loss of morale can be a problem: half the battle is giving clients the confidence to believe they can carry on.

I check a client's ability to carry out tasks – strength and co-ordination – and their mental capabilities such as memory and recall. We also assess the support available at home, from school or work, and the local community.

Physiotherapy

Physiotherapists are trained to alleviate physical problems, especially those of the nervous, muscular, skeletal and respiratory systems.

In an outpatients department, physios treat spine and joint problems, accidents and sports injuries. In intensive care wards, they help keep limbs mobile and chests clear. They advise mothers-to-be on posture and strengthening exercises. Elderly people are helped to maintain mobility and retain independence, or rehabilitated after accidents. Physiotherapy can also help sufferers of arthritis or Parkinson's disease. Physiotherapists support victims of strokes, people who are mentally ill and people with learning difficulties, with exercise, sport and recreation. In orthopaedics, they assist after spinal operations, joint replacement or accidents. In hospices, they help patients cope with cancer, AIDS and motor neurone disease. In paediatrics, they support children with a range of mental and physical disabilities.

Chartered physiotherapists also work in sports clinics and centres, football clubs, voluntary organizations, private health clinics and companies trying to prevent industrial injuries. They also have an important health education role.

Keith – physiotherapist

I really like my job. I don't have any problem getting out of bed in the morning!

Keith Lambert is a self-employed physiotherapist working in private practice. Keith earns around £25,000 per year.

I qualified several years ago. I had to work for two years after registration for the NHS and then I worked in a private hospital. The private health sector has the same qualification requirements as any NHS institution.

Later I was chief physio for a football team in south London. That was good; the equipment and facilities were first rate, and it was a real challenge dealing with some very serious injuries. After a few years, however, I decided I wanted to go back into private practice. I now work in a clinic on a self-employed basis, specializing in sports injuries and spinal problems.

As a physiotherapist, there's an obligation to follow professional development courses. I'm currently studying for a Master's degree at Leeds University. The degree is modular, and spread over five years. Working in private practice means I can pay for the course and travel up to Leeds for each module. Ultimately I want to teach.

Apart from the sports injuries, who all seem to come in on Monday after kicking lumps out of each other in the park over the weekend, I'm seeing many more people with postural problems associated with sitting at computers.

Physiotherapists have to be easy going and good problem solvers, and that, I think, makes them nice people to work with.

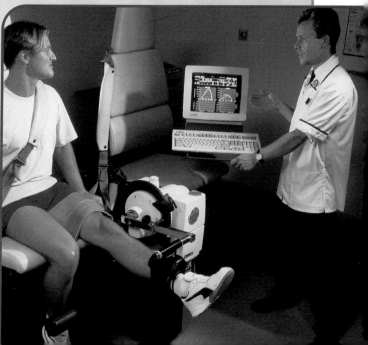

⭐ *The sports physiotherapist devises individual programmes to help athletes recover from injury.*

Speech and language therapy

The power to communicate complex ideas distinguishes us from every other creature on earth. Language is a glue that binds society; it is vital to our relationships with others.

Many people have communication problems – a consequence of stroke, disability, cancer, head injury, hearing loss, cleft palate and psychiatric disorders. **Speech and language therapists (SLTs)** work with people of all ages who might have difficulty producing and using speech sounds, understanding or using language, a stammer or other voice problem. Many SLTs also work with people who have swallowing difficulties. Speech and language therapists support parents and carers and other professionals such as teachers, nurses and doctors.

There is much more to speech, and therefore speech therapy, than you might think. Each sound is made up of an intricate combination of tongue, teeth, lips, breath and vocal cords movements. Many of these we learn as toddlers, by listening to and imitating parents, brothers and sisters. Speech therapists teach skills many of us take for granted. People who are profoundly deaf, for example, learn to speak by completely different means. Similarly, problems of the palate and tongue frustrate the ability to make many verbal sounds, and new ways must be taught, often after surgery.

Most SLTs are employed by the NHS or educational service. Some work for charities or in private practice. Registered SLTs work in community health centres, hospitals, mainstream and special schools, assessment units and day centres, and in a client's own home.

There is a considerable demand for SLTs, with many opportunities for bilingual speech and language therapists.

⭐ *Speech therapy helps people of all ages communicate more successfully. This boy has a repaired cleft palate.*

Nutrition and dietetics

For most people, 'diet' means watching the calories, but there's more to it than that. **Nutritionists** study food and the way our bodies use it. They also examine the relationship between diet, health and disease.

Public health nutrition promotes healthy eating to reduce diet-related illnesses like heart disease. Registered Public Health Nutritionists (RPHNutr) complete a human nutrition degree and three years in public health nutrition. Some colleges now offer public health nutrition courses.

Food, glorious food!

To stay healthy, we should:

- Eat five servings of fruit and vegetables every day
- Eat wholemeal bread, brown rice, bean and pulses
- Include fish, olive oil, nuts and seeds in our diet
- Limit consumption of animals fats.

Dietitians are trained to explain nutrition to people. State registered dietitians (SRDs) give dietary advice in hospitals and the community. SRDs often run clinics for people who need specialist counselling; these include kidney patients, diabetics and individuals with food allergies. Dietitians also educate doctors, nurses and health professionals about nutrition. SRDs in intensive care wards calculate the nutrition for people fed through tubes and ensure the feeding equipment is working. Rather than being kept in hospital, less seriously ill people are usually sent home. SRDs in the community help and advise them in their homes. SRDs also visit schools and nursing homes to talk to students or staff about nutrition.

CONSIDER THIS...

THERE ARE OPENINGS FOR NUTRITIONISTS AND DIETITIANS OUTSIDE THE HEALTH SERVICE IN:

- FOOD MANUFACTURING AND RETAIL
- FOOD SCIENCE AND TECHNOLOGY
- JOURNALISM
- GOVERNMENT
- EDUCATION

Gill – Sports Nutritionist

Not long ago, footballers drank tea at half-time – which makes dehydration worse!

Gill Donlon works with athletes competing in a wide range of sports. Gill is self-employed and earns about £17–19,000 per year. Her income fluctuates depending on the demand for her services.

I've always been interested in sport. I completed a degree in Applied Human Nutrition and did a thesis on Sport and Nutrition. My clients now include triathletes, swimmers, runners, jockeys, dancers, sprinters and boxers. I'm also a member of the National Sports Medicine Institute.

Sports nutrition has developed in recent years. The two most important issues are hydration and ensuring we have enough energy to train and compete. Myths persist; some strength athletes think they must eat protein, others believe the secret of a good diet is cutting out fat. It's important to get the right balance of essential fats, carbohydrates and proteins.

I'm concerned about athletes with eating disorders. It affects both men and women, especially dancers, runners, boxers and jockeys. They don't realize the long-term risks or that their performances will suffer.

Several of my fellow students are SRDs, others are working as journalists or in sports nutrition full-time.

I think my job is great; I work with really interesting people, who take my advice very seriously, in a science that is developing all the time.

Working in dentistry

'Open wide!'

For most people, regular visits to the **dentist** are essential. To eat, talk and smile without discomfort or embarrassment is important to us all. For the British Dental Association, the focus of dental care is prevention. If decay occurs, however, the dental team have sophisticated techniques to treat it.

Dentists are taught to recognize problems affecting the mouth and teeth. As well as clinical skills, a dentist must be sensitive to a patient's anxieties.

Dental nurses are essential. They assist the dentist – changing instruments, removing water and saliva from the patient's mouth, sterilizing instruments and preparing materials for fillings. Dental nurses might process X-ray pictures, record information about the patient and do stock control. They often work at reception – talking to clients, booking appointments and taking money.

⭐ *Dentists check for problems affecting the mouth and teeth and have sophisticated techniques to treat them.*

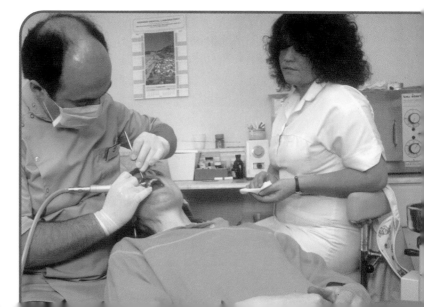

Dep – Dentist

I know some people are scared of the dentist. But sometimes I see someone with a mouth full of bad teeth and I want to shake them and say, 'You could have a perfect smile!'

Dep Gupta is a dentist in a small but busy dental practice in Manchester. At the moment Dep earns around £22,000 per year. As a practice owner, however, he could expect to earn a lot more.

Like most dentists, after dental school I decided I wanted to be a general dental practitioner (GDP). I did a year's vocational training and entered general practice as an associate – a self-employed dentist in a practice owned by two partners. I did my vocational training here. When I finished, they had a vacancy and took me on, so I must have done all right. I've been here ever since.

Day-to-day work is varied. No two mouths are the same and even check-ups are unique. During an average day, I'll do check-ups, fillings, make impressions for dentures, bridges and crowns, measure and fit braces, fit crowns and do extractions. There are a surprising number of emergencies, and yes, people sometimes do come in with scarves wrapped around their heads!

There's an emphasis on surgical hygiene these days, and we wear full-face visors. We're also very aware of gum disease and problems of the jaw, and can refer people to orthodontists for specialist treatment if necessary.

The practice tries to keep long opening hours and have at least one dentist available at all times between 8.00 am through to 8.00 pm. It fits in with our clients' lives, and I think they appreciate it. It's good for me too; I can come in early, do a full day's work in the surgery and still have most of the afternoon free!

I am thinking of becoming a practice owner one day. At the moment, I'm happy here; it's a relaxed practice with a good atmosphere, and I like the work.

A **dental hygienist** is concerned with education as well as clinical care. A hygienist works closely with the dentist and examines the patient before recommending treatment. The hygienist teaches people how to look after teeth and gums. This is not just about cleaning teeth – which is more complicated than we realize! It is also about motivation and technique. Hygienists explain the importance of diet for healthy teeth and gums and are trained to remove deposits using hand scalers or ultrasonic scalers. They are also trained to apply fluoride and fissure sealants to teeth.

A **dental therapist** works exclusively within the community and hospital service caring for children, expectant mothers and patients with special needs. Like dental hygienists, they do clinical and education work. Dental therapists are trained to clean and scale, apply sealants, administer local anaesthetics, extract children's teeth and do simple fillings.

Dental technicians make a range of dental appliances including crowns, bridges, orthodontic devices and dentures. They need technical proficiency and dexterity, and some artistic flair!

Don't forget your toothbrush!

There's a huge market in dental products – and that's not just toothpaste! Everything from abrasives to X-ray equipment, laboratory tools to impression materials must be made, warehoused, sold and shipped. Specialist manufacturers and distributors understand the unique requirements of dentists, dental technicians, orthodontists and dental therapists.

Dental specialities

Some dentists train for several years to become **hospital dentists** specializing in oral surgery, restorative dentistry, children's dentistry and orthodontics. Patients are referred to hospitals by a GDP or general practitioner. Hospital dentists usually see serious cases often involving complex medical problems or facial injuries.

Orthodontics focuses on the growth process of the head. An **orthodontist** works with people, especially children, who have hereditary or birth problems that have affected the way their heads and mouths develop. Orthodontists usually lead a multidisciplinary team including facial and plastic surgeons, paediatricians, speech therapists and ear, nose and throat (ENT) specialists.

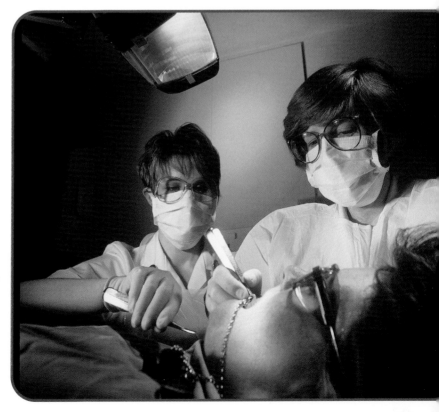

⭐ Dental surgery is used to deal with more complicated conditions.

Ophthalmology and optometry

It has been said that the eyes are the windows of the soul. They capture the imagination of painters, poets and writers more than any other human feature.

The eye is a miracle of nature's engineering, but with such a delicate organ things do go wrong. Sight tests identify a range of conditions, and are carried out regularly at school. Adults are recommended to have one every three years.

Our eyes and the tissue around them can be affected by many conditions. An **ophthalmologist** combines the diagnostic skills of a physician with the technical skills of a micro-surgeon. In recent years, ophthalmologists have pioneered new technology and conditions such as cataracts – once a common cause of blindness – can now be treated. Now that once-impossible operations can be performed with only local anaesthetic, patients can be seen as day cases and go home after surgery. A general ophthalmologist will remove cataracts, correct squints and perform glaucoma surgery.

Given the fragile nature of the eye, it's not surprising that emergencies are common. These are usually dealt with in an A & E department's Eye Room, which is staffed by **junior ophthalmologists** and trained **nurse practitioners**.

Consultant ophthalmologists select sub-specialities including corneal disease, correcting nerve damage, working on cancers of the eye and children's ophthalmology. Because many eye conditions also affect other tissues, ophthalmologists form part of multidisciplinary teams of dermatologists, plastic surgeons, neurosurgeons, ear, nose and throat (ENT) and maxillofacial surgeons and paediatricians.

Other professionals also care for our eyes. **Ophthalmic nurses** provide specialist support in eye clinics, wards and operating theatres. Some train to become nurse practitioners.

An **orthoptist** specializes in the problems of ocular movement, binocular vision and children's sight, working as part of a team in the eye unit or as a community orthoptist.

Many **optometrists** (better known as **opticians**) practise in the high street, testing clients and prescribing and dispensing spectacles. Many also work full- or part-time in the Hospital Eye Service fitting special glasses, complex contact lenses and low vision aids.

Some people lose both eye and surrounding tissue as a consequence of illness or injury. To disguise the effect, **ocular prosthetists** manufacture and fit both ocular prostheses – false eyes – and oculofacial prostheses.

Ophthalmic photographers use photographic and video technology to record eye complaints and treatments.

Opticians perform eye tests and prescribe appropriate spectacles where necessary.

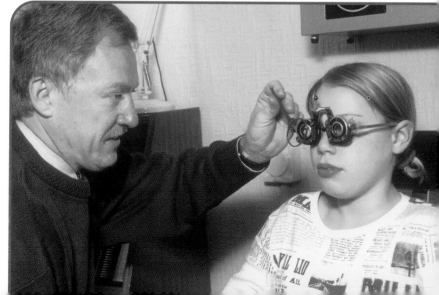

Complementary and alternative medicine

Complementary medicine supplements mainstream medicine. Public interest in complementary medicine has grown, and it is now on the medical school curriculum. The effectiveness of some treatments is supported by observation rather than scientific proof. This does not mean they are wrong – many medical practices began like this. However, some therapies remain little more than mysticism; cures have not been demonstrated and claims of success are anecdotal.

Caution

If you are thinking about a career in complementary medicine make sure you follow an accredited course. Several organizations are trying to raise standards of practice and of practitioners: there are a few charlatans out there! The BMA wants to stop people without training from practising. The British Complementary Medicine Association agrees, arguing for integration between complementary and mainstream medicine.

Acupuncture has been used in China for over 3000 years. Steel pins are inserted into specific points around the body to change the flow of energy through the body until balance is restored. Migraine, anxiety, poor circulation, high blood pressure and asthma are claimed to benefit. The British Acupuncture Council (BAcC) represents qualified acupuncturists. All members undergo at least two-years full-time training.

Osteopathy and **chiropractic therapy** both claim many ailments are caused by misalignments of the skeletal system or muscular spasm. These are corrected by manipulation of the spine, neck and pelvis and joints of the shoulders, arms and legs.

Naturopathy is based more on maintaining health than curing disease. Health and the immune system are strengthened through good nutrition, lifestyle changes, hydrotherapy – hot and cold water – and exercise. The British College of Naturopathy and Osteopathy offers several courses. Modules include Sports Science, the Physiology of Exercise, Human Physiology and Anatomy.

Homeopathy, devised by Samuel Hahnemann, a German physician, in the 19th Century, is based on the idea that 'like cures like' and 'drug activity is enhanced by dilution'. The belief is that if a drug in large doses causes symptoms similar to those of an illness then it can be used to treat that illness, if diluted. It is popular and has credibility amongst some medical professionals. The Royal London Homoeopathic Hospital runs courses to meet the special needs of doctors, dentists, professions allied to medicine (PAMs), nurses and midwives, pharmacists and clinical psychologists.

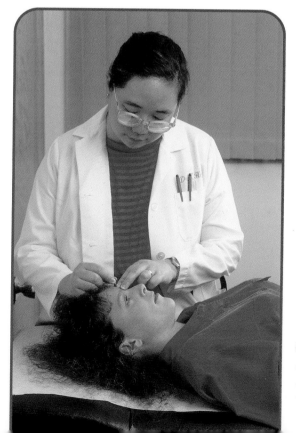

Hypnotherapy uses hypnotism to deal with medical and psychological conditions. **Reflexology** uses pressure to points on the hands and feet to stimulate the reflexes and the body's own healing processes. **Herbalists** use remedies from natural plant sources to treat a range of complaints, including eczema and psoriasis, and digestive disorders.

⭐ *Acupuncture originated in China and is now practised worldwide.*

Getting into healthcare

Thinking ahead

You will have realized that most careers in healthcare demand an understanding of science, in particular Chemistry and Biology. However, good interpersonal and communication skills are essential for the modern healthcare professional. You must be able to work closely with others, and your ability to communicate is important – whether explaining, discussing, diagnosing or making suggestions. The growing emphasis on health promotion gives even greater weight to these skills; the art of persuasion can save lives.

Vocational courses

General National Vocational Qualifications (General Scottish Vocational Qualifications in Scotland) develop skills and understanding of broad work areas. **Intermediate GNVQs** are equivalent to four GCSEs at grades A*–C. **Advanced GNVQs** are aimed at 16–19-year olds. Appropriate GNVQs include:
● GNVQ Health and Social Care
● GNVQ Science
Three grades are awarded: pass, merit or distinction.

National Vocational Qualifications or **Scottish Vocational Qualifications** are job-specific and can be followed to professional levels. NVQs/SVQs are accredited and monitored by the Qualifications and Curriculum Authority (QCA) and the Scottish Qualifications Authority (SQA).

NVQs divide into framework areas. 'Providing health, social and protective services' options include: Blood Donor Support, Diagnostic and Therapeutic Support, Dialysis Support, Health Care – Technical Cardiology, Health Care – Physiological Measurement; Audiology, Neurophysiology, and Respiratory, Operating Department Practice and Operating Department Support.

Choosing the right qualifications

Several programmes can be followed at school and/or college. As well as GCSEs and A levels, there are vocational alternatives. Options include:

- GCSEs and A levels
- NVQs/SVQs in Healthcare
- GNVQs in Health and Care, and Science
- BTEC (EDEXCEL) Firsts and Nationals in Health and Social Care, and Science
- BTEC (EDEXCEL) HND/HNC courses in Health and Science
- Modern Apprenticeships in Health and Administration.
(Remember: GNVQ, GCSE, A level and NVQ units can be mixed.)

Remember, medical schools still regard A levels as the 'Gold Standard' of academic achievement! If you believe you have the ability to be a doctor, it is vital to take the right academic route; most medical schools want excellent GCSEs and A levels, and accept no substitutes. All insist candidates have A level Chemistry and normally require a second in either Maths, Physics or Biology. Most medical schools expect applicants to offer a minimum of AAB grades at A level. In Scotland, Scottish medical schools accept a minimum of five Highers – AAABB. The majority of medical schools do not accept BTEC or GNVQ in place of A levels. A quarter will accept Advanced GNVQ, preferably in Science (distinction) plus an A level in Chemistry. HNCs and HNDs are also accepted by some medical schools.

Vocational qualifications are accepted by many nursing colleges and centres specializing in the training of therapists, scientists and technicians.

However, whatever area of healthcare you want to enter, check which qualifications are acceptable to the college or training body you plan to enrol into!

National Traineeships and **Modern Apprenticeships** help school leavers gain skills and qualifications while working. National Traineeships offer training to NVQ Level 2 in Health and Community Care. Modern Apprenticeships take trainees at least to NVQ Level 3, and can open the way to university. Modern Apprenticeships are available in Operating Department Practice, Health and Social Care and Physiological Measurement.

BTEC Firsts and **Nationals** are also work-related qualifications. Like many GNVQs and NVQs, they are administered by the Edexcel Foundation. Firsts are approximately equivalent to Intermediate GNVQ or NVQ Level 2. A National Certificate is equivalent to A levels, an Advanced GNVQ or NVQ level 3.

BTEC courses can be followed to **Higher National Diploma/Certificate** (HND/HNC) level. HND/HNCs are recognized by several professional bodies including the Chartered Society of Physiotherapy, the College of Occupational Therapists, the College of Radiographers, the Council for Professions Supplementary to Medicine, the Institutes of Biology, Biomedical Sciences and Health Services Management, the Royal College of Speech and Language Therapists and the UK Central Council for Nursing, Midwifery and Health visiting. For information on BTEC courses visit the Edexcel web site. (See pages 56–60 for details of all useful web sites.) Your school Careers' Library or Careers' adviser will have information. Course lists can also be obtained from QCA Publications, the QCA web site, the DFEE web site, and from the Training Information Service.

State registration

All professions in healthcare have governing bodies which oversee training standards and register qualified staff. Before beginning a course, make sure it is recognized by a relevant professional board. It is impossible to follow a career in the National Health Service or the private sector without state registration.

Training to be a doctor

Be realistic: in 1997, 13,000 people applied to 27 medical schools in the UK and only 5000 were accepted. Medical schools demand excellent grades at GCSE and A level. They also look for interpersonal skills, outside interests – in art, literature, sport – good health, and a realistic view of the medical profession.

During their five-year course, medical students study Anatomy, Physiology, Biochemistry, Psychology, Pathology and Pharmacology. They also do clinical work. After medical school, a graduate works for a year as a house officer then registers with the General Medical Council. They then spend two years as a senior house officer, before beginning higher specialist training.

Nursing and midwifery

Both the **Diploma of Higher Education in Nursing (DipHE Nursing)** and a **nursing degree** involve theory and nursing practice. Midwives also train to diploma or degree level. Midwifery is studied in hospital and the community. Minimum qualifications are five GCSEs (grade C or above). English is essential, Maths is preferred and Integrated/Double Science very useful. Most degree programmes require at least two A levels, preferably sciences. Alternatives include NVQ/SVQs at Level 3, Advanced GNVQ/GSVQs and BTEC qualifications. Communication is a key skill for nurses and midwives. They must be able to explain themselves to patients and other health professionals.

Specialist courses administered by United Kingdom Central Council (UKCC) help qualified nurses develop their careers. Staff often rotate between nursing areas to consolidate experience.

Medical Laboratory Scientific Officers

The Institute of Biomedical Science require a degree for most biomedical jobs, including MLSOs. University requirements vary, but usually include A level Biology and Chemistry and GCSE Maths or equivalents. The best degrees are those designed for the profession, such as Biomedical Science. Some courses are part-time; a trainee can study while working in a laboratory. A candidate must also complete one to two years' training in an approved labratory and take **Council for Professions Supplementary to Medicine (CPSM)** examinations for registration.

Radiography

Information about careers in both diagnostic and therapeutic radiography is available from **The College of Radiographers,** and NHS Careers publish a leaflet (HSC11). Entry requirements are usually three GCSEs (C or above) including English and Maths and two A levels, or equivalents – HND, GNVQ in Science or Health Studies.

Mental health

Psychiatrists first qualify as doctors. Qualification as a psychiatrist requires three years of study and training in one of six psychiatric fields.

Information about psychotherapy is available from the **British Association of Psychotherapists.**

Chartered Psychologists take a Psychology degree and a post-graduate course accredited by the **British Psychological Society.**

Occupational therapy

Degree courses last three or four years, part-time courses are available. Most require five GCSEs and three A Levels. Alternatives include BTEC (EDEXCEL) HND or Advanced GNVQ (Science or Health and Social Care).

Chiropody

Information about careers in chiropody (podiatry) is available from the Society of **Chiropodists and Podiatrists,** the **Institute of Chiropodists and Podiatrists,** and *NHS Careers.*

Physiotherapy

Students interested in physiotherapy should visit a physiotherapist at work. Hospital physiotherapy departments often hold open days. A physiotherapist completes a degree validated by the **Chartered Society of Physiotherapy** and the **CPSM.** Colleges emphasize A level Science and competition means conditional offers are often higher than the minimum. Alternatives include HND (Science) with distinction/merit in all units or Advanced GNVQ/ GSVQ. (Most institutions require a science A level.)

Speech and language therapy

Recognized qualifications are three- or four-year degree courses or two-year postgraduate degree accredited by the **Royal College of Speech and Language Therapists (RCSLT).** The practical element combines weekly placements with longer block placements in schools, health clinics and hospitals. Entry qualifications are five GCSEs and three A levels or four Scottish Highers. GCSE passes in English, a second language, Maths and a science are an advantage.

Dietitians and nutritionists

Applicants for degrees need at least two A levels preferably Chemistry and another science subject. GNVQ/GSVQ Advanced or HND (Science) with merit pass in Chemistry may be acceptable. Courses include practical training in hospital and health centres.

Dentistry

Dentists take a five-year degree which includes theoretical and practical training. Like medicine, academic requirements are high. Courses lead to a **Bachelor's degree** (either **BDS** or **BChD**).

Dental nurses can study part-time for the **National Certificate of Dental Nursing**. There are full-time courses in most dental hospitals. A dental hygienist is often a qualified dental nurse. Training lasts for two years at a **School of Hygiene** attached to a dental hospital. Some colleges offer combined **Dental Therapy/Dental Hygiene** courses.

Most technicians complete a five-year day-release course while employed at a dental laboratory. There are BTEC (EDEXCEL) HND Science (Dental Technology) courses and GNVQ/GSVQ Advanced courses.

Complementary medicine

Before beginning any training in complementary medicine, you must find out about:
- the quality of training
- the cost
- how widely recognized the qualifications are
- does qualification enable you to register and obtain the necessary insurance to practice?

Information about a number of complementary therapies including hypnotherapy and reflexology is available from the **Institute of Complementary Medicine.**

All members of the **British Acupuncture Council (BAcC)** train for at least two years full time. Courses are monitored by the British Acupuncture Accreditation Board (BAAB). There are currently four accredited colleges and three awaiting accreditation.

The **British College of Naturopathy and Osteopathy** run courses including a four-year option leading to practitioner status. Modules include Sports Science, Human Physiology and Anatomy. Normal entry requirements are three A levels – including Chemistry and Biology– and five GCSEs including English and Maths. Equivalent qualifications such as BTEC are accepted. Information about chiropractic training is available from the **British Chiropractic Association.**

The **Society of Homoeopaths** can provide a list of colleges running recognized homoeopathy courses. Information on aromatherapy is available from the **International Federation of Aromatherapists.** Students interested in herbal medicine should contact the **National Institute of Medical Herbalists or the School of Phytotherapy (Herbal Medicine).**

Health management

The **NHS Management Training Scheme** is a two-year course to train candidates for management throughout the NHS. Applicants should have a degree or an equivalent professional qualification, be persuasive communicators able to see the 'big picture', and have management potential.

Useful information, addresses & contacts

General

NHS Careers
PO Box 376
Bristol BS99 3EY
Tel: 0845 60 60 655
www.nhscareers.nhs.uk

NHS Careers information leaflets offer help for nurses and midwives, radiographers, scientists, biochemists, geneticists, engineers, microbiologists, technicians, medical illustrators, pharmacists, dental support staff, physiotherapists, orthoptists, occupational therapists, speech and language therapists, dietitians, Medical Laboratory Scientific Officers, clinical laboratory support staff, clinical psychologists, chiropodists, art, music and drama therapists, orthotists and prosthetists.

NHS Management Training Scheme
National Office
The Manor House
260 Eccleshall Road South
Sheffield S11 9PS
Tel: 0114 226 3000
www.nhs-mtsandmesol.demon.co.uk

Education and training

Qualifications and Curriculum Authority
29 Bolton Street
London W1Y 7PD
Tel: 020 7509 5556 (Enquiry line)
www.qca.org.uk

Northern Ireland – QCA-NI
2nd Floor
Glendinning House
6 Murray Street
Belfast BT1 6DN
Tel: 028 9033 0706

Accac/QCA Authority for Wales
Castle Building
Womanby Street
Cardiff CF1 9SX
Tel: 029 2037 5400

QCA Publications
PO Box 99 Sudbury
Suffolk CO10 6SN
Tel: 01787 88444

Scottish Qualifications Authority
Hanover House
24 Douglas Street
Glasgow G2 7NQ
Tel: 0141 248 7900
www.sca.org.uk

For information on the National
Traineeships and the Modern
Apprenticeships contact your local Careers
Service or Training and Enterprise Council
or:

The Training for Young People Division
Department for Education and Employment
Room W4D
Moorfoot
Sheffield S1 4PQ
Tel: 0114 259 3573
www.open.gov.uk/dfee/ntrintro.htm
www.open.gov.uk/dfee/mapintro.htm

Or contact:

Training Information Service
PO Box 200
Timothy's Bridge Road
Stratford-upon-Avon CV37 9HY
Tel: 0345 66 55 88

EDEXCEL Foundation (BTEC)
Stewart House
32 Russell Square
London WC1B 5DN
Tel: 020 7393 4500
www.edexcel/org.uk

Medicine (including research)

British Medical Association
BMA House
Tavistock House
London WC1H 9JP
Tel: 020 7387 4499.
www.bma.org.uk

Royal College of Anaesthetists
48-49 Russell Square
London WC1B 4JY
Tel: 020 7813 1900
www.rcoa.ac.uk

Royal College of Surgeons of England
35-43 Lincoln's Inn Fields
London WC2A 3PN
Tel: 020 7973 2100
www.rcseng.ac.uk

Royal College of Psychiatrists
17 Belgrave Square
London SW1X 8PG
Tel: 020 7235 2351
www.rcpsych.ac.uk

Royal College of General Practitioners
14 Princes Gate
Hyde Park
London SW7 1PU
Tel: 020 7581 3232
www.rcgp.org.uk

Royal College of Physicians
11 St Andrews Place
Regent's Park
London NW1 4LE
Tel: 020 7935 1174
www.rcplondon.ac.uk

The Royal College of Physicians includes
bodies overseeing Accident and Emergency,
Medicine, Cardiology, Dermatology,
Endocrinology, General (Internal) Medicine,
Geriatric Medicine, Neurology, Renal
Medicine, Respiratory Medicine, and
Rheumatology and Rehabilitation,
Occupational Medicine.

British Association of Dermatologists
19 Fitzroy Square
London W1P 5HQ
Tel: 020 7383 0266
www.skinhealth.co.uk

Royal College of Pathologists
2 Carlton House Terrace
London SW1Y 5AF
Tel: 020 7930 5861
www.rcpath.org

Faculty of Public Health Medicine
4 St Andrews Place
London NW1 4LB
Tel: 020 7935 0243
www.fphm.org.uk

Royal Institute of Public Health and Hygiene
28 Portland Place
London W1N 4DE
Tel: 020 7580 2731
www.riphh.org.uk

Medical Research Council
20 Park Crescent
London W1N 4AL
Tel: 020 7636 5422
www.mrc.ac.uk

The Wellcome Trust
183 Euston Road
London NW1 2BE
Tel: 020 7611 8888
www.wellcome.ac.uk

Forensic Science Society
Clarke House
18a Mount Parade
Harrogate HG1 1BX
Tel: 01423 506068
www.demon.co.uk/forensic

Nursing and midwifery

NHS Careers
PO Box 376
Bristol BS99 3EY
Tel: 0845 60 60 655
www.nhscareers.nhs.uk

Welsh National Board for Nursing Midwifery and Health Visiting
2nd Floor
Golate House
101 St Mary Street
Cardiff CF1 1DX
Tel: 029 2026 1400

National Board for Nursing Midwifery and Health Visiting for Scotland
Careers Information Service
22 Queen Street
Edinburgh EH2 1NT
Tel: 0131 247 2096

School of Nursing and Midwifery Registry Office
The Queen's University of Belfast
1-3 College Park East
Belfast BT7 1LQ
Tel: 028 9027 3745

For nursing or midwifery diploma courses in England:

Nursing and Midwives Admissions Service
Rosehill
New Barn Lane
Cheltenham
Gloucestershire GL52 3LZ
Tel: 01242 544949

For information on degree programmes contact:

UCAS
Rosehill
New Barn Lane
Cheltenham
Gloucestershire GL52 3LZ
Tel: 01242 544961

Professions allied to medicine

The Council for Professions Supplementary to Medicine
184 Kennington Park Road
London SE11 4BU
Tel: 020 7582 0866
www.cpsm.org.uk

Institute of Biomedical Sciences
12 Coldbath Square
London EC1R 5HL
Tel: 020 7713 0214
www.ibms.org

College of Occupational Therapists
106-114 Borough High Street
London SE1 1LB
Tel: 020 7450 2332.
www.cot.co.uk

The British Psychological Society
St Andrews House
48 Princess Road East
Leicester LE1 7DR
Tel: 0116 254 9568
www.bps.org.uk

British Association of Psychotherapists
37 Mapesbury Road
London NW2 4HJ
Tel: 020 8452 9823
www.bap-psychotherapy.org

Chartered Society of Physiotherapy
14 Bedford Row
London WC1R 4ED
Tel: 020 7306 6666
www.csp.org.uk

The Society and College of Radiographers
2 Carriage Row
183 Eversholt Street
London NW1 1BU
Tel: 020 7391 4500
Not yet online.

Royal College of Speech and Language Therapists
7 Bath Place
Rivington Street
London EC2A 3DR
Tel: 020 7613 3855
www.rcslt.org

Society of Chiropodists and Podiatrists
53 Welbeck Street
London W1M 7HE
Tel: 020 7486 3381
www.feetforlife.org

Institute of Chiropodists and Podiatrists
27 Wright Street
Southport
Merseyside PR9 0TL
Tel: 01704 546141
www.inst-chiropodist.org.uk

British Nutrition Foundation
High Holborn House
52-54 High Holborn
London WC1V 6RQ
Tel: 020 7404 6504
www.nutrition.org.uk

The British Dietetic Association
5th Floor
Elizabeth House
22 Suffolk Street
Queensway
Birmingham B1 1LS
Tel: 0121 616 4900
www.bda.uk.com

Nutrition Society and
The Institute of Food Science and Technology, both at
10 Cambridge Court
210 Shepherds Bush Road
London W6 7NJ
Tel: 020 7602 0228
www.nutsoc.org.uk

Institute of Biology
20-22 Queensberry Place
London SW7 2DZ
Tel: 020 7581 8333
www.primex.co.uk/iob

Complementary and alternative medicine

Institute for Complementary Medicine Association
249 Fosse Road South
Leicester LE3 1AE
Tel: 0116 282 5511
www.icmedicine.co.uk

British College of Naturopathy and Osteopathy
Lief House
3 Sumpter Close
120-122 Finchley Road
London NW3 5HR
Tel: 020 7435 6464
www.bcno.org.uk

British Chiropractic Association
Blagrave House
17 Blagrave Street
Reading RG1 1QB
Tel: 0118 950 5950
www.chiropractic-uk.co.uk

British Acupuncture Council
63 Jeddo Road
London W12 9HQ
Tel; 020 8735 0400
www.acupuncture.org.uk

The Association of Reflexologists
27 Old Gloucester Street
London WC1N 3XX
Tel: 0870 5673320
www.reflexology.org/aor

The Society of Homoeopaths
2 Artizan Road
Northampton NN1 4HU
Tel: 01604 621400
www.homoeopathy.org.uk

National Institute of Medical Herbalists
56 Longbrook Street
Exeter EX4 6AH
Tel: 01392 426022
www.btinternet.com/~nimh

College of Phytotherapy (Herbal Medicine)
Bucksteep Manor
Bodle Street Green
Near Hailsham
East Sussex BM27 4RJ
Tel: 01323 834800
www.blazeweb.com/phytotherapy

International Federation of Aromatherapists
Stamford House
2-4 Chiswick High Road
London W4 1TH
Tel: 020 8742 2605
www.int-fed-aromatherapy.co.uk

Dentistry

British Dental Association
64 Wimpole Street
London W1M 8AL
Tel: 020 7935 0875
www.bda-dentistry.org.uk

Ophthalmology

Royal College of Ophthalmologists
17 Cornwall Terrace
London NW1 4QW
Tel: 020 7935 0702
www.rcophth.ac.uk

Get the jargon – a glossary of healthcare terms

accident and emergency (A & E) hospital department where casualties are admitted and treated

acute lymphoblastic leukaemia blood cancer which produces a tumour made up of blood cells in the brain

anaesthetic chemical substance producing insensitivity to pain

antenatal events taking place before birth

basic specialist training (BST) training undertaken by a senior house officer

bone marrow inside of the bone where all white blood cells are produced

cardiology study of the heart

cardiothoracic surgery surgery of the heart and chest

chemical pathology science of body chemistry

clinical psychologist psychologist who deals with problems of the mind and mental illness, stress and anxiety

computer tomography (CT) advanced body scanning system

consultant doctor who has been given the Certificate of completion of Specialist Training (CCST)

counselling psychologist psychologist who is trained to help clients help themselves to alleviate anxiety, depression, etc

deoxyribonucleic acid (DNA) chemical units making up genes of most living organisms

dietician person trained to give advice on food and diet to clients, often experienced in the special dietary needs of people with a variety of illnesses

endocrinology glandular medicine

forensic pathology legal pathology

gene part of every chromosome

gene sequence arrangement of genes in every DNA

general practice working of a general practitioner in the community

genetics study of genes and the genetic causes of illness

geriatric care care for elderly people

geriatric medicine medical care of the illnesses associated with elderly people

Golden Hour the short period after injury or the onset of illness when a patient's survival chances are at their highest

graduate person who has completed and passed their first degree

haematology study of blood disorders

haemophilia condition where blood fails to clot normally

higher specialist training (HST) training undertaken by a specialist registrar

Hippocratic Oath code of ethics devised by Hippocrates

histocompatibility and immunogenetics study of organ transplants and tissue matching

histopathology study of diseased tissue

house officer pre-registered medical school graduate working the first year in hospital

Human Genome Project project to map out the whole human gene sequence

immunology study of the immune system

intensive care one-to-one nursing for very seriously ill patients

magnetic resonance imaging (MRI) advanced scanning system

malignancy harmful cancerous tumour made up of uncontrolled cell growth

microbiology study of diseases caused by bacteria and funguses

molecular and cellular medicine medicine dealing with diseases at a molecular or cellular level

neonatal care care of new-born babies

neurology treatment of the brain and nerves

neuropathlogy diseases of the nervous system

neurosurgery in the brain and nerovous system

nurse practitioner nurse with additional training and responsibilities

nutritionist expert in food and nutrition

obstetrics and gynaecology medical care of childbirth and the diseases of women

occupational medicine medicine that deals with work-place health and work-related illnesses

occupational therapy therapy to develop independence and life skills in people with mental and physical difficulties

oncology specialism in the treatment of cancer

ophthalmic nurse nurse specializing in treatment of the eyes

ophthalmic photographers photographers specializing in using video and photographic techniques to identify a variety of eye conditions

ophthalmologist eye specialist

oral and maxillofacial mouth, jaw and facial surgery

orthopaedic surgery surgery dealing with bone and muscle

paediatrics speciality relating to diseases in children.

paramedics highly trained accident and emergency personnel

pathology study of the disease process

physiotherapist specialist in physical mobility and movement

positron emission tomography (PET) advanced scanning system

postgraduate person who has followed an additional programme of study after passing a first degree

post-mortem after-death examination to determine cause of death

post-natal events taking place after birth

professions allied to medicine (PAMs) physiotherapists, radiographers, speech and language therapists, psychologists, technicians, etc.

psychiatry speciality relating to mental illness

psychotherapist person who uses a one-to-one relationship with clients to work out problems and change behaviour

radiography use of X-ray and other imaging/scanning equipment for diagnosis and therapeutic purposes

radiotherapy use of radiation as a curative agent

senior house officer registered doctor undertaking basic specialist training

social worker person who supports the work of PAMs with people suffering ill-health, mental health problems, people at risk, supporting mentally ill people in the community

specialist registrar doctor undertaking HST

speech and language therapist therapist dealing with language difficulties and sound

stem cells cells from the base of the brain that contain all the genetic information of an individual

thesis extended research paper written as part of a degree or postgraduate degree programme

toxicology study of poison

transfusion medicine medicine dealing with blood and blood products

triage system of prioritizing casualties according to seriousness of injuries

vascular surgery surgery dealing with arteries and blood supply.

virology Study of disease caused by viruses

X-ray ray from powerful radioactive source used to create images of internal organs and bones

Index